Cursive Handwriting Practice Book

Children's Reading & Writing Education Books

All Rights reserved. No part of this book may be reproduced or used in any way or form or by any means whether electronic or mechanical, this means that you cannot record or photocopy any material ideas or tips that are provided in this book

Copyright 2016

Trace the letters of the alphabet and then write your own.

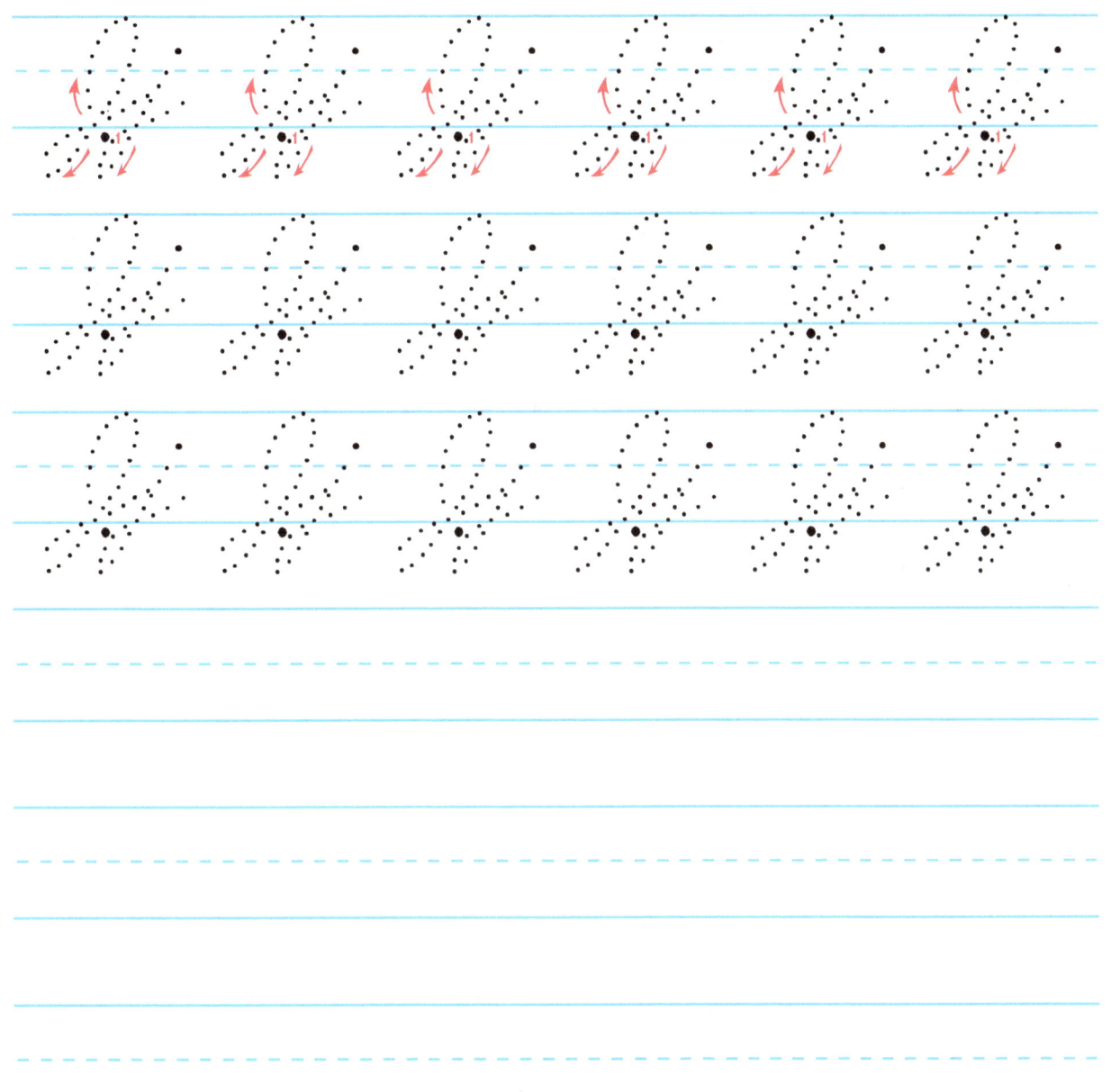

Mm Mm Mm Mm

Mm Mm Mm Mm

Mm Mm Mm Mm

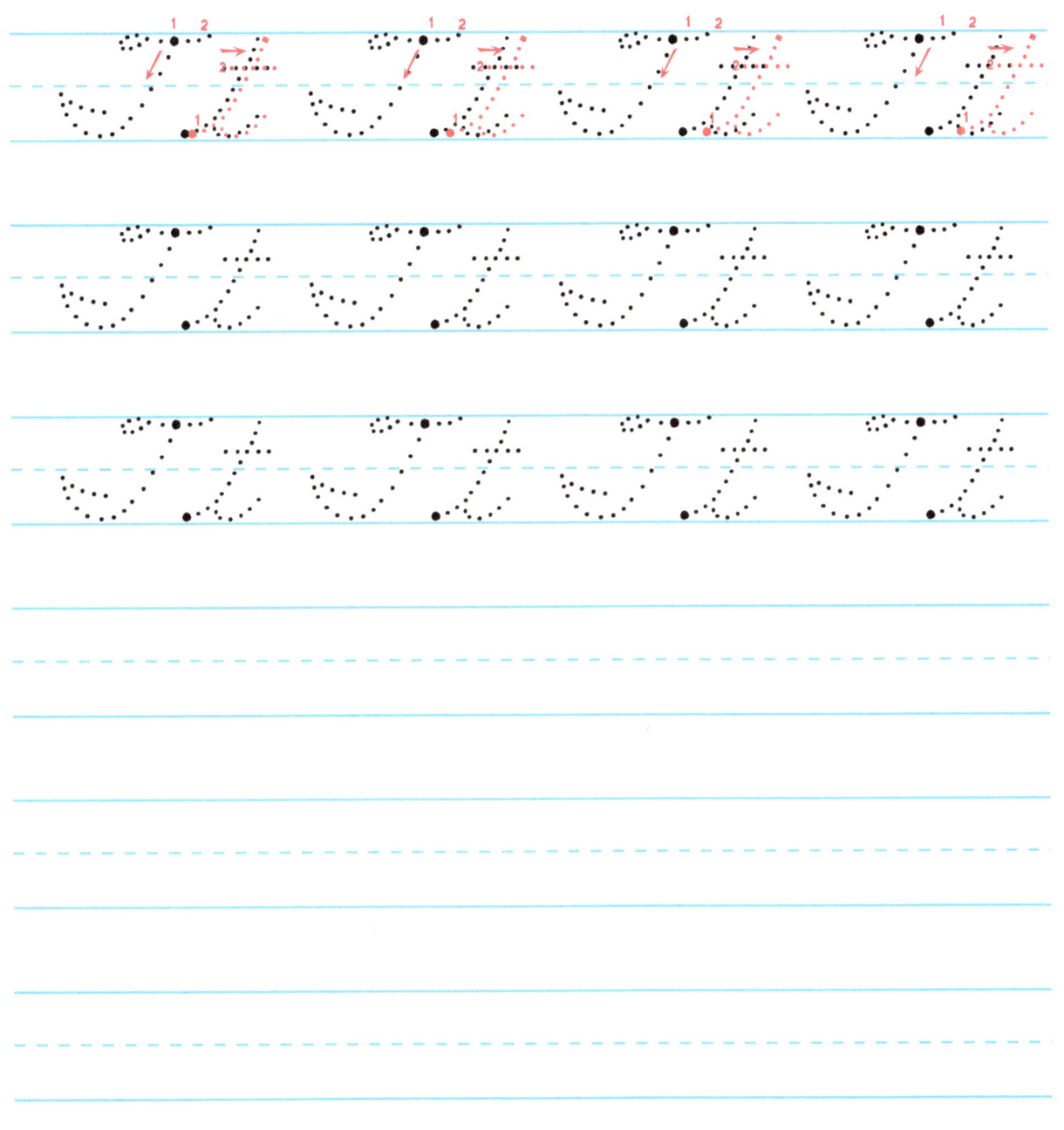

Ww Ww Ww Ww

Ww Ww Ww Ww

Ww Ww Ww Ww

Trace the words and then write your own.

about

about

act

age

baby

boy

cub

carry

cloud

dance

day

dog

game

gift

glad

hair

hand

hat

keep

king

knock

lucky

last

love

mud

map

mud

mom

mat

mom

own

at

me

page

pink

pen

www.ingramcontent.com/pod-product-compliance
Lightning Source LLC
LaVergne TN
LVHW061321060426
835507LV00019B/2258